MW00629789

# PRAISE FC

"Have you questioned your calling? Concerned for the future years of your career based upon the stamina you have left at the end of your day? Well Colleen has been there. Infusing her authentic voice, real stories and practical strategies *The Burn Book* will take you on a journey that will make you laugh, cry and love the calling to teach again."

*—Jessica Cabeen*
*Award Winning Principal,*
*Author and Speaker*

"Are you complacently going through the motions? Have you gotten too comfortable in your classroom? Does your status quo risk being set in stone? Then it's time to let educator Colleen Schmit ignite something bigger and better in you. Don't miss this hot new guide to rediscovering your why; with every page come words of wisdom and intriguing insight to spark your resolve to keep burnout at bay while you stretch and grow to become your best version of yourself with every intentional choice."

*—Barbara Gruener,*
*Author of "What's Under Your Cape?"*
*Author of "The Corner on Character" Blog*

"*The Burn Book* is a quick read that every teacher needs to have within reach throughout their educational journey! Throughout the book, Colleen Schmit provides warning signs and solutions for those that are dangerously close to burning out! She hits the nail on the head when she states, 'change forces growth'. This is something we must all remember. Oh, and if by the end of this book you don't have a #workwife already, you will be running to find one or five!"

—*Katy Phinney*
*Pre-K Program Director*
*Co-moderator of #ECEChat*

"If you are an educator, you will experience burnout. It's ok. Take a deep breath and know you are not alone. *The Burn Book* is authentic and validating. It helps you rediscover the WHY behind your career, so you can continue to shine brightly for your students instead of burning out in a blaze of glory. When you inevitably find yourself lost under a mountain of things other people tell you are important, this quick read helps you find YOU."

—*Carol Houser*
*Nebraska Association for the Education of Young Children Board Member, Director of James R. Russell Child Development Center, Omaha*

"Colleen Schmit is not afraid to talk about the elephants in the room that leave so many teachers feeling burned out. She offers real solutions for getting out of the rut of negativity that can so easily creep in if you are not careful. This book will help you identify symptoms of teacher burnout and help you rekindle your love and passion for teaching."

*—Nancy Alvarez*
*Principal*
*#ECEChat Co-moderator*

"This book is so needed for the hard-working teachers in the field. It's easy to feel alone and downtrodden, and this book gives real support to help navigate this tough, but important career!"

*—Mary-Margaret Gardiner*
*Former Director, Teacher, VA QRIS,*
*Past President for Virginia AEYC*

"Teacher, are you on the verge of burnout or are already experiencing full-blown burnout? Then *The Burn Book* has found you at just the right time! Through this gem of a book, Colleen Schmit candidly explores the eight primary reasons teachers experience burnout and practically delivers key strategies to extinguish the burn for good, transforming what can be a very stressful time for any teacher into a new lease on one's calling. In the book, Colleen's transparently shares her own experience with burnout, helping you, reader, to feel and know that you are not alone and can do something about it. We've all been there, at one time or another, and *The Burn Book* will honestly deliver the 'how to' needed to extinguish teacher burnout."

—*Heidi Veal*
*Early Childhood Programs Administrator*
*#ECEChat Co-moderator*

# THE

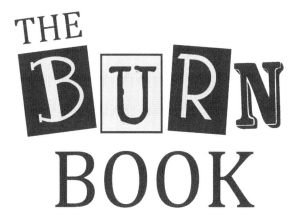

# BOOK

**8** Key Strategies to *Recognize*
and *Extinguish* Teacher Burnout

## Colleen Schmit

Omaha, Nebraska

THE BURN BOOK
8 KEY STRATEGIES TO RECOGNIZE
AND EXTINGUISH TEACHER BURNOUT

Four Monkeys Press books are available from your favorite bookseller or from www.FourMonkeysPress.com

Paperback ISBN: 978-0-9973508-0-7
Mobi ISBN: 978-0-9973508-4-5
EPUB ISBN: 978-0-9973508-5-2

Library of Congress Cataloging Number: 2019900474
Cataloging in Publication data on file with the publisher.

Cover and Layout Design: Rachel Moore

Printed in the USA

10 9 8 7 6 5 4 3 2 1

Dedicated to my Mom,
who told me to go get it.

# CONTENTS

# BURN, BABY BURN

A Journey to Burnout

This September marked my 15th year working in education. FIFTEEN! I blinked and it's here. While teaching, the days went fast and the years went even faster. For whatever reason, this anniversary has me reflecting more than ever on my career in education. I recently switched career paths and the self-reflection fairy visited me again—in fact she has been nagging at me every night this week. So I have finally given in and decided to let her win. Self-reflection can sometimes be a scary thing. When you hold up the mirror it is not only the warm fuzzies and beautiful moments that stare back at you. In true self-reflection you will also see large pores, dark circles, and age spots. But these aren't necessarily bad things to have to look at! Everyone has them. I believe in strength-based and positive reflections, but I also see the value in looking at the areas where you need to grow. You need rain to get roses.

My self-reflective journey led me to write my first book: *Crisscross Applesauce and Shut the Hell Up: 10 Reflective Lessons for New and Seasoned Teachers.* Writing this little book was freeing and liberating well beyond any expectations I had going in. What started as journal entries of me venting and reflecting eventually turned into a book intended to guide teachers through basic self-reflective practices. If I am being totally honest…that first book was more beneficial for me than anyone else. I was the one in major need of a mirror. The self-reflection happened because I actually took a break to breathe and broke up with teaching.

Looking back, the reason for the break was simple—I ran out of gas. Burnout hit.

Burnout is an interesting thing…you don't realize it has found you while you are in it. When you are finally able to step away from the situation and look back, that is when you will be able to label what was happening. I never thought I would leave teaching. In my mind being a teacher was my vocation, my calling. It was what I was built to do.

But I was on a quick path to becoming a very crusty old schoolmarm. I was frustrated with the demands of my job. After eight years in the classroom, I had become COMPLETELY resistant to any new curriculum implementation or ideas my district would provide. I was engaging in gossip and had an overall negative attitude. I still loved my students and their families, but it wasn't the same as in my early years. I wasn't giving the same amount of enthusiasm and zest that I once had as a 23-year-old girl. I was no longer focused on building relationships with my students but more concerned about whether or not I was keeping up with rigorous expectations. It was time to go.

Not only had I become overwhelmed because of job demands and crusty because of my resistance to change, but after my sixth year of teaching I had my second child. Going from having one child to two children was a gamechanger. It knocked me square on my butt. Mostly I just couldn't keep up anymore. When I was teaching and had only my firstborn I already felt like I could barely keep my head above the water, but I was able to keep going and maintain the facade that I could do it all. After having number two…fuuugeeetaboutit. I was no longer able to keep up with this illusion of being a super teacher and more importantly a super mama. Because that was what it was…an illusion. If you were to walk into my classroom it was beautifully decorated and organized. All of my paperwork was done and neat. My students were quiet and working. I looked good on paper. Same with my home life…if you were to walk into my home it was clean. My kids were dressed in the latest GAP outfit (often matching). Every Christmas card showed the perfect family. My Facebook and social media pictures showed nothing but cuteness and sweet. But this isn't exactly reality. There are struggles and warts in every family and every home. Too often, we feel the need to hide the warts by putting out this picture that everything is perfect and rose petals all the time.

The reality of the situation was that I would work with little people all day and come home to my own little people and not have much left to give. Dora the Explorer did a lot of my mothering. I would plop the kids onto the couch and lay beside them like a zombie woman. I was there in body but not in spirit. Our dinners consisted mainly of dinosaur chicken nuggets or mini corndogs. I was in survival mode. When I was at school I was only trying to tick things off my To Do list. I wanted to do the bare minimum to get me through the day. I mostly lost track of my **WHY** I became a teacher. I was only focused on my **HOW** I can survive and still make it appear like I am great. Needless to say, I was unhappy both at home and at school. One of my very favorite colloquialisms is, "If mama ain't happy, nobody is happy." The same goes for teacher, "If teacher ain't happy, nobody is happy". I just wasn't in a great place and a change was needed.

## NOTE

I am not saying that you can't be an effective teacher and an effective mama at the same time. YES, you can. But what I am saying is this... we need to start talking about the real challenges that working moms are facing (Sorry dudes. Yes, men have challenges too, but here I am addressing the ladies). ESPECIALLY those working in education. I am going to go into more detail with this topic later in the book so hang tight. This is an important conversation we need to start having and we need to quit acting like everything is fine when the house is actually on fire.

Leaving was not something I took lightly. It really did break my heart, but I am thankful every day for being strong enough to go. It was scary but at the same time essential. Where did I go, you ask? I found a job working part-time as an early childhood program evaluator at the University of Nebraska Medical Center. I worked at UNMC for seven years and learned a crazy amount about early childhood education during that time. When I was teaching, I did not realize how many options exist out there to still serve kids/families outside of the traditional classroom setting. *Hint.* *Hint* Reader… if you are starting to feel the burn consider looking around and discovering your options. As a program evaluator I was still serving, just in a different way. While working at UNMC (and peeing basically whenever I wanted—hugest perk) …I reflected. I breathed. I wrote a dang book. I found myself again. I realized my new mission and started fulfilling it.

And that new mission is to help educators avoid some of the same strife and growing pains that I went through. Above all else, I am an advocate for kids. That has always been my **WHY**. Even when I mostly lost sight of that **WHY** it was still there in the very back of my mind. My **HOW** is different now and probably (and hopefully) will continue to change down the road. I am currently an advocate for children by helping teachers. I know that if I can reach you, I can reach many, many kids by extension. I never, ever, ever, ever intended to be a public speaker. Speaking to teachers is scary as hell. I can talk to a group of 40 six-year-olds without breaking a sweat but put me in a room with my peers and I freak out. I also never, ever, ever, ever, intended to be an author. My words are plain. I am not fancy. Without a doubt you will catch at least 48 grammatical errors in this book. The reason I overcame these fears is because I believe my mission is truly helping kids through reaching teachers. My **HOW** has changed. My **WHY** is the same.

This book is short and sweet. That is intentional. Your time is valuable, and I want you to actually read this book. My goal with this quick read is to help educators recognize the signs of burnout and suggest strategies to combat the burn. Yes…self-reflection will still be a part of this but more so than that what I really hope you will take away from this book are strategies to recognize when burnout is hitting and an understanding of what steps to take next. We need to start having more conversations about what burnout is and not feel ashamed or embarrassed to reach out for help. Teacher, let me help you!

## DISCLAIMER 1

This book is not full of statistics and facts. There are very few fancy links to years of research. If you are looking for that type of read this ain't it. I am going to talk to you like I talk to my sister... blunt, with a small amount of cussing while offering solid advice.

## DISCLAIMER 2

Please note that some of the examples and recommendations you will find in this book are drawn heavily from my own experience as a kindergarten teacher. But please don't dismiss or move past those lessons just because you are teaching older kiddos. Take the spirit of what I am saying and mold it to apply more directly to your own grade level. I promise you won't be disappointed in the results.

"If teacher ain't happy, nobody is happy."

# SETTING OFF THE FIRE ALARM

## Conforming to an Institution

1

I graduated from undergrad with a degree in elementary education and a specialization in early childhood education from The University of Nebraska at Omaha. UNO has a strong teacher's college. In particular, they have an outstanding early childhood education program. As a student I learned a lot about theorists (e.g. Piaget, Vygotsky, Maslow, Bloom, Froebel). We spent a lot of time delving into Developmentally Appropriate Practices for young kids—what they looked like and how to implement them. When I student taught I was placed with an amazing veteran teacher who was the perfect mix of constructivist and behaviorist. All in all, my undergrad experience was stellar, and I felt ready to take on the world. So…. when I first began in the classroom, I taught the way I was taught to teach.

With my background in early childhood, I knew that young kids needed to move. I allowed my students to wiggle and fidget while seated on the carpet or at their tables. If kids were on their knees during a read-aloud but everyone could still see, then I did not correct that behavior. We danced often and moved A LOT. Not only were we moving but we were also talking. "Give me 5" and "SHHHHHHH" were not frequent words out of my mouth during my early years. I wanted to elicit the ideas that were in my students' little brains. I needed to know what they knew so I knew where we needed to go. Again…during a read-aloud if a child shouted out a response or a question (and it pertained to what we were doing) I did not interrupt their learning with, "Ope! We must remember to raise our hands" because that type of constant interruption can stifle creative thinking.

NOW before I go any further and you get your torches and pitchforks out.... YES! We must have behavioral expectations in the classroom. They are the structure, the backbone of your room. However, what you must also consider is this—do your classroom expectations meet the needs and abilities of your students? If you've ever spent any significant amount of time with a five-year-old, you will know that sitting still and being quiet for long periods of time are not exactly their strengths! Having an expectation that a five-year-old should sit still and quiet for more than 5-10 minutes is simply not reasonable.

My kids were moving. They were talking. They were also choosing. Choosing what we would study, how long we would spend on the topic, and what they wanted to learn from this topic. I used the project approach to help guide my instruction. This type of project work follows the interests of your students and integrates all subjects together. It prevents silo teaching. Math, reading, science, social studies, etc. are all incorporated into the project. I will be totally honest with you… the project approach does require extended effort, but the results are WORTH it. What the project approach supports is creative thinking as opposed to encouraging cookie cutter thinkers. The project approach allows students to have choice in their learning. It is what creates lifelong learners and researchers. It's a lot of work on the teacher's end (and sometimes tricky for type A teachers to get on board with) but the results are amazing. My experience has been that the project approach (along with a teacher who focuses on fun and joy) is what makes learning meaningful and school fun. In my opinion, it is what the teacher is there for—to guide and support learning, not to dictate and demand.

So here I was as a newbie. Just like Mary Tyler Moore, I too wanted to change the world with my smile. I had a hippie dippy, developmentally appropriate style of teaching and I really LOVED my job and how I was doing it. But guess who didn't?... many of my peers, coworkers, and members of my leadership team, that's who. The first-grade teacher would see my kindergartners sitting in the hall waiting to use the bathroom and the kids would be talking and laughing (but not in a loud way that was interrupting learning in other classrooms) and she would have a fit and teacher shame me in front of my students. "Oh no. Mrs. Schmit. Your kindergartners don't know the school rules. I am going to have to reteach them everything when they come to first grade," she would whine. I definitely did not like how that felt so I would correct my kiddos and say, "Give me five Kindergarten." They would. And then they'd proceed to sit quietly and with frowns on their faces looking miserable and bored.

The music teacher would come into my classroom and she'd bring instruments and books and all sorts of fun things to engage with. My kids would be excited. They'd be on their knees or trying to talk to her about what she had brought into our room (because that was the type of environment we had set up in the room) and Mrs. Music Teacher would lose it, "Kindergarten! You do NOT sit on your knees and you do not talk out without raising your hand! Give me FIIIIIVE. Mrs. Schmit… your students owe me time. At the end of music class today everyone will put their heads down on their tables for five minutes for a time-out." Well… it was one thing for me to be teacher shamed by the first-grade teacher in the hall. It was another thing for my kids to get punished for the behavioral expectations that I had set. I could feel a quiver inside of me that maybe the Developmentally Appropriate Practices I was implementing were a bunch of foo foo nonsense and really couldn't work in an actual classroom.

The final straw that really broke the camel's back was when I began to receive feedback from my own grade level team. I loved my grade level team. They were kind and had lots of nuggets to always share with me. In September in Nebraska the weather starts to get cooler. With this change the creepy crawlers start to venture into the classroom to hide from the sometimes-chilly Nebraska nights. Crickets, spiders, grasshoppers, and ants would venture in the classroom. I will generalize here and say five-year-olds are intrinsically curious about these critters so their arrival into our classroom would naturally lead to some sort of project on bugs.

When my grade level team found out that I was doing a project on insects and we weren't talking about apples in my room they had some words for me, "We had already long-range planned our year before you even came. We have tied all the standards into a month-long apple unit. You MUST teach apples. Look! We even have all of the copies already made that we will use."

*But my kids don't care about apples! They want to know if crickets sleep at night.*

"We need to be consistent. You must do apples."

I wanted to be a team player. I wanted to be seen as a master teacher. I loved my job. I loved my school. I loved my coworkers. I especially LOVED my students and their families. The feedback I was receiving did not feel good and definitely did not make me feel like I was fitting in. I began to conform to the institution. I became the queen of rigid expectations. I stopped implementing the project approach the way I was taught and tried to make it fit into a long-range planning model. Long-range planning project work basically takes a lot of choice out for your students. This meant I wasn't teaching through projects anymore. It meant I was teaching through themes. My kids no longer shared freely on the carpet. I was a drill sergeant who consistently interrupted their sharing out with my classroom expectations. When I conformed I received nothing but praise from my peers and administration.

Every review or observation I received was perfect. I fit the mold. My principals would send other teachers from around the district into my classroom so they could see how I was teaching. So they could emulate my practice. So it could spread.

## DISCLAIMER 1

I truly believe that the feedback I received from my coworkers and administration could have happened at any school in any district in any city. These types of institutional expectations have been happening for years. My coworkers were not terrible teachers or nasty people. Everyone was simply doing their best with what they knew. My first year of teaching was in 2003. The pendulum of education is starting to swing again. 15 years ago looked different. We were so focused on NO CHILD LEFT BEHIND that we often lost sight of what our mission really was.

## DISCLAIMER 2

No one is responsible for me
conforming and changing my
practices except for yours truly.
I do wish that as a 23-year-
old girl I would have had enough
voice to explain to my peers why
I was teaching the way I was.
I wasn't brave enough to share
that voice. I didn't have it. I do
now. And I am happy to share
it with anyone who will listen.
I feel it is part of my duty to
spread my burnout message loud
and clear. Hence...why I wrote
this book and most likely why you
decided to read it!

# RECOGNIZING WHEN YOU'RE FEELING THE BURN OF CONFORMING

Many of you may be thinking…*Okay. Yes! This sounds familiar. This is my story too. Pretty much this exact same scenario happened to me during my early years of teaching. I changed many of my practices to fit into a school.* I receive that feedback after every single professional development session I have led for the past two years, "That happened to me. Thank you for sharing that story! That is my story too." The trickiest part about teacher burnout is labeling your feelings while you are on fire. I remember feeling like I was just barely able to keep my head above the water when teaching, so taking the time to reflect and ponder wasn't high on my list. I sure wish I would have had the sense to stop, look, and reflect. But I didn't. Below are warning signs that you too may be conforming to an institution and not necessarily doing what is best for your students:

🔥 You change your classroom expectations to match an entire school. (Again, yes school expectations are important but we must also meet the abilities and needs of our kids).

🔥 You have given the same worksheets to your students year after year no matter what varied academic and social skills they possess.

🔥 You roll through lessons based on a pacing guide. If there is a lack of student understanding you ignore it and continue with future lessons versus taking time to reteach or using a new strategy to ensure that your students are truly learning.

🔥 You value long-range planning more than you value following students' interests and giving them voice and choice in their learning.

🔥 You teach in silos. Content and new information is isolated and not connected for students (e.g. teaching social studies one quarter and science the next. No connection is happening).

- 🔥 You hear a small voice in the back of your head that is telling you the practices happening at your school are not the best for kids, but you chose to ignore that little voice.

- 🔥 You have forgotten best practices you learned in undergrad or are choosing to ignore those practices.

# HOW TO EXTINGUISH THE FLAME

It is most likely that you can check off at least a few, if not many, of the warning signs above. If you are reflecting enough to recognize some of this burn, congratulations! Seeing it is the hardest part. Here's what to do next…

🔥 Go back to your roots. Start having fun with teaching again. Remember **WHY** you are in the classroom. Your job is to excite, support, and guide learning. Start igniting the flame for your students. It feels good! When you are excited about teaching the kids magically become excited about learning.

🔥 Revisit the theorists. Put Piaget in your pocket and be prepared to pull him out. When you have others question the way you are teaching you must be able to back it up with a reason. This is especially true when trying to defend Developmentally Appropriate Practices in early childhood. Somewhere along the line we have forgotten that third grade is technically a part of early childhood.

🔥 Invite other teachers into your room to observe your style and ask for their feedback. Be prepared and open to hear the good, the bad, and the ugly. Make the assumption that the feedback they are giving is laced with good intentions.

🔥 Observe other teachers and try new styles and modalities of teaching!

🔥 Break free from silo teaching. Start trying to integrate subjects and content. Make as many connections as you can for your students.

🔥 STOP mass producing plans from year to year. Every year you get a new crew of kids. Their interests are never the same. Get creative and allow your lessons to flow from students' interests while continuing to follow your content standards.

Choosing not to conform does not mean that you chose to be a jerk or teach in isolation. It means you advocate for your students by continuing to do what is best for your kids. Not conforming also does not mean you become resistant to change…which leads us to our next burn….

"Do your classroom and school expectations meet the needs and abilities of your students?"

# WE DIDN'T START THE FIRE

## Resisting Change

We have just discussed how important it is to stay true to what you know is good for kids. YES! Not conforming to an institution is extremely important to prevent burnout but I don't want you to confuse not conforming with being inflexible and resisting change. The only thing constant with education is that there WILL be change. The pendulum of current trends will swing from one side to the other. We didn't start this fire. In the words of Billy Joel: "It was always burning since the world's been turning." Change happens whether you like it or not, Teacher. Change is not a dirty word.

When I conformed to fit the institution of my school I was praised. Every single evaluation I received from my administration (which followed the district's format guidelines to a tee) was perfect.

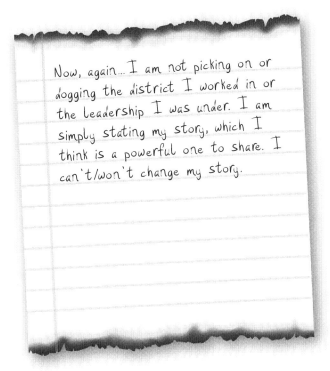

Now, again... I am not picking on or dogging the district I worked in or the leadership I was under. I am simply stating my story, which I think is a powerful one to share. I can't/won't change my story.

With each perfect evaluation I internalized that feedback to mean that I was doing exactly what the district was looking for. I had a belief that what I was doing was the right way to do things. Maybe the only way to do things. This came back to bite me in the butt.

When change came knocking on my classroom door (like it always will) I quickly slammed that door. *Why do I need to try to implement that curriculum? I already know what I am doing. I don't need to go to a PD session during the last week of school. This meeting doesn't apply to me. I am doing everything right. I don't have time to do anything new.* Sheesh. Talk about a nasty, conceited way of thinking, right? I spoke earlier of the fact that when you hold up the mirror of reflection you see some of the ugly. Well, here is a big part of my ugly. I resisted any sort of change that came my way. I had become used to teaching out of my file folders. While at school, I wanted to check items off my list. Get my copies made. Plan two weeks ahead. Go through the motions. Change did not fit nicely into the equation.

When it boils down to it, what change really is about is growth. Change forces growth. That was the component I was missing when I became resistant. I no longer cared to grow as a teacher. I was comfortable where I was at and I was being praised for what I was doing. Not only did I not care to grow or learn new things, but I also became very hesitant to ask for help around my fifth year of teaching. I was embarrassed and too full of pride to admit that I still needed help, especially when that help involved not knowing how to handle certain student behaviors or classroom management issues. I was now seen as a master teacher in my district. How could I admit I still didn't know what I was doing? I had pre-service teachers sent to my room to do their student teaching practicums. Different teachers from the district visited my class to observe my teaching and learn from it. I must know what I am doing. I must not need to change or grow. This line of thinking was a big mistake and led me even further into the flames.

# RECOGNIZING WHEN YOU'RE FEELING THE BURN OF RESISTANCE

So how do you know when you are resistant to change? Again, this is hard to recognize within ourselves when we are in the middle of doing the resisting. The biggest hint that you may be resisting change is a NO CAN DO attitude. Below are attitude warnings and other early indicators that you have decided to stop growing as an educator.

- You are closed-minded to leaning new ways of teaching or learning about current trends.

- You are annoyed with every professional development opportunity you have been asked or required to attend.

- You always believe you know what you are doing and continue to teach with cookie cutter lessons that you have used from year to year.

- You are unwilling to even consider switching to a new grade level, content, school, district, or position.

- You sit at staff meetings with a frown on your face and scoff when it is suggested that the school or team will implement a new routine, procedure, or curriculum.

- You have an overall attitude of "I can't. I won't. I don't wanna. I am not gonna."

# HOW TO EXTINGUISH THE FLAMES

Oof…some of these burn reflections may be very hard to handle, but if you are really being 100 percent honest with yourself there's a good chance you will notice a few of these characteristics in you. Look, I get it. Teaching is hard. It is a demanding job that is more than just a job. It is more than just a career. It is an optimistic act of service for our youth, for the future. It seems as though everyone has an opinion about how you should teach and why our schools are "failing". When you read my list of warning signs on resisting change you may be thinking: *"I want to try new things, but it is the district's fault for overloading me with unreasonable expectations." "I can't even complete the plans I am already required to do. How can I add something new?"* I hear you, Teacher. I have been there, remember? I am not trying to discredit how hard your job is or how important your role is in our world. Teaching is challenging. Point blank.

Recently I have returned to the classroom as a substitute teacher and very quickly I am remembering how challenging teaching really is. There are four primary reasons for my return to the classroom: (1) I have missed the kids and teaching SO MUCH! (2) I need to keep up on current trends and practices. (3) I need the street cred. No one wants to listen to someone tell them how to do their job who isn't actually (in some form) DOING THEIR JOB! (4) For the last 2 years I have been working as a consultant and offering professional development to teachers. In order to effectively work with and help teachers, I need to experience first-hand what they are experiencing in today's classrooms. I have been talking all the talk. I needed to prove to myself that I can still walk the walk.

Let me tell you… returning to the classroom has kicked me square in my booty. It is HARD! I have basically forgotten how to do everything, but I am open to learning this time around. My attitude is very different. I actually ask for help. I have been humbled. I have learned the only one in charge of your attitude is YOU. You can decide how you will handle the winds of change because they will blow. It is a fact. Your only hope for maintaining some of your joy and sanity as a teacher is to be able to go with the flow (at least a little bit)!

🔥 Take responsibility for your attitude. Also understand that you cannot control the attitude of those around you. You can only be accountable for your own attitude.

🔥 Be open to saying yes instead of always resisting new ideas with a big fat NO. Now I am not saying you should always say yes to everything. Saying, "NO." can be a huge form of self-care (and in certain instances NO is simply the right answer). I am merely suggesting that you at least be open-minded to new things.

🔥 Have fun while learning new strategies or curriculum. Finding a buddy or your Work Wife* can make your whole teaching journey much more enjoyable. (*More to come on what the heck a Work Wife is and why you should get married in Chapter 3.)

🔥 If you try something new and it isn't working, don't just complain about it in the teachers' lounge. "Ugh. They have forced us to do this new Science curriculum and it is so lame. I don't have time for it." Instead, change your attitude about why it could help your students. If you've tried it and it really is just not working, make a list of suggestions on how it could better meet the needs of your kids and try to adjust!

🔥 GO WITH THE DANG FLOW. Truly. Be open to trying new things. Let the pendulum swing and hop on to enjoy the ride.

Change will be a constant component of your job as a teacher. It is not going anywhere. But you have all the power when it comes to deciding how you yourself will handle change when it does come. Resisting change doesn't make it go away. Ultimately, resisting change will only make you feel miserable, mad, and nasty. Would you rather be a bitter critter or have fun? I once had a principal who ended morning announcements each day with the saying, "Make it a great day or not. The choice is yours." What are you going to choose, Teacher?

> "The only thing constant with education is that there will be change."

# STANDING OUTSIDE THE FIRE

## Teaching in Isolation

Have you gone to the chapel? Are you married at work? Do you have a Boo? As a teacher you need a special someone in your work life. That is why I highly recommend you find your Work Wife (or husband, Work Wife is just more fun to say). Your ability to enjoy your job depends on it. Just make sure you marry well.

When I first began teaching I was assigned a mentor. He was a veteran teacher on my kindergarten team. We clicked instantly because of his ability to tell it like it was, his love for the kids, and how he could add humor to any situation. He became my Work Spouse. Don't get it twisted. No funny business was happening. My real spouse at home—the one I actually took vows with—heard about my Work Wife often. We were good work friends who could count on each other. A Work Wife has your back.

Here are a few job requirements of a Work Wife or how you can identify if you have one:

- 🔥 They pick up an extra copy of a handout for you from the staff meeting you missed.

- 🔥 They snag a donut for you from the lounge before they're all gone.

- 🔥 They listen to you vent (not gossip) and help you find the good in a situation.

- 🔥 They provide guidance on how to support students' behavioral or academic issues. They do this without judging.

- 🔥 They build you up and can also give you some truth telling when you need it.

⟡ They let you borrow any craft item you need from their craft cupboard.

I do not know how I would have gotten through my first few years without my Work Wife. He made teaching so much more fun. He could talk me into doing crazy lessons that I would never think to do on my own (e.g. make homemade ice cream with 40 kindergartners). Did we agree on everything all of the time? Hellz nos! We often fought and bickered like siblings. But he was fun. He made me feel good about teaching. He made coming to work enjoyable. After my third year of teaching, my Work Wife transferred schools. At that time, I was well on my way to conforming and changing my practices to fit into an institution. The joy was leaving my job and the transfer of my buddy didn't help with that situation. I never married again. At least not in the same way I had those first few years. That was a big mistake. I began isolating myself from my peers and coworkers. The weird part was I was team teaching. I began teaching in settings that required collaboration (ie room sharing, teaching in a dual language setting, and job-sharing a kindergarten position). I had teaching partners that I HAD to collaborate with. My partners were lovely people and great teachers. I am sure I could have remarried, and my teaching life would have been much more enjoyable. Instead, all my focus was on my To-Do lists and what I needed to do to conform to my institution. I was becoming a full-on crust bucket, and in the process I had forgotten all about the value of a Work Wife.

## RECOGNIZING WHEN YOU ARE FEELING THE BURN OF ISOLATION

Teaching in isolation may be easy to recognize but hard to accept. You may need to check a little bit of your pride and ego at the door when you look to see if you are teaching in collaboration or in isolation. Isolated teaching may seem like it has its benefits. You can do everything the way you want. You don't need to take the time to help or support others. No advice or opinions are given to you. You're the boss. These are short term benefits that really end up stoking the fire of burnout in the long run. Are you collaborating or isolating? You better check yourself before you wreck yourself. See the list below.

- You dislike working with a grade level or content team.

- Staff meetings that require team building or "get to know you" activities really grind your gears.

- You shut your door every day during plan time and only focus on your own plans and checklists.

- Most days you eat alone. (*Alone time is fine for recharging your battery but always eating alone or isolating yourself is no good).

- After-school social functions with your coworkers are viewed as a waste of your time.

- You have an attitude of "I am not here to make friends."

🔥 You don't share stellar lessons or strategies that have worked for you with your colleagues. You want to compete, so you keep the good lessons to yourself in order to make you look better.

🔥 When you need help, you refuse to ask for it and continue trying to navigate on your own.

# HOW TO
# EXTINGUISH
# THE FLAMES

Teaching is a demanding job. "It takes a village to raise a child." This saying is not based on nothing. It is for real and applies to teaching too. It takes a village to teach children. We need each other. Collaboration between teachers not only supports the teacher and helps to prevent burnout but collaboration also directly benefits the students. There have been many studies that prove quality collaboration between teachers directly correlates to an increase of emotional and academic learning outcomes for kids! Here is the only part of this book where I will get all researchy on you…

From 2010-2012 9,000 teachers from Miami Public Schools participated in a research study on the effects of teacher collaboration. The teachers were surveyed and the team of researchers sought to answer a variety of questions in relation to collaboration. The question I found most interesting was: Is the quality of teacher collaboration associated with student achievement and teacher improvement with experience? Guess what the answer was in a nutshell…yes! Not only did collaboration improve teaching practices and result in higher levels of student achievement but the quality of the types of collaboration mattered too **(Ronfeldt, M., Farmer, S., McQueen, K., & Grissom, J. (2015)**. Collaborating with your coworkers will benefit and help you, and it will help your students! Isn't that the point? That is why you are teaching. You don't need to go it alone. Here are a few strategies to extinguish the flames of isolation and fan the flames of collaboration.

- Develop meaningful and authentic relationships with your coworkers.

🔥 SHARE! Share ideas that are working in your classroom. Sharing is not being braggy. Sharing is being an advocate for kids by spreading what works.

🔥 Partner with another classroom and plan engaging and fun activities to do together.

🔥 Go to at least some social functions outside of school. If your team doesn't have social functions outside of school, consider organizing one!

🔥 Change your attitude about fluff team building activities. I am not saying you need to love every icebreaker or "get to know you" game. Just remember the intent of these activities is to help you team build and develop relationships.

🔥 Ask for help. Asking for help doesn't mean you are a bad teacher. It actually is quite the opposite. Asking for help means you are still growing as an educator and aren't too prideful to remember that.

🔥 Find your Work Wife. Your Work Wife does not necessarily have to be someone who teaches the same grade level as you or the same content. If you want, you can be a polygamist and have more than one Work Wife.

Isolated teaching may seem to be the easy route to go, but the ones who will ultimately suffer are the kids. Sharing effective practices, asking for help when needed, and feeling cared for at work will make you a happier teacher. Remember: "If teacher ain't happy, nobody is happy". Find your friends and your community. Get married and find at least one Work Wife. Just make sure you marry well and choose a spouse focused on building you up and spreading positivity throughout the school…. which brings us to our next burn: Setting the School on Fire with Negativity.

> "Collaborating with your coworkers will not only help you, but help your students too!"

# ADDING FUEL TO THE FIRE

## Setting the School on Fire with Negativity

Let's get a little comfortable with the uncomfortable. Can we talk about the elephant in the teacher's lounge? Negativity. It is in every school you could visit. The level varies but negativity is present everywhere. Cliques, gossip, ostracizing each other, and talking negatively about the kids you serve and their families are all negative behaviors that are far too common in schools. Obviously, these behaviors aren't only happening in the lounge (although the lounge tends to be a breeding ground for this type of junk). They happen everywhere.

Passive-aggressive behaviors from educators are commonplace in many schools. For example, one person wearing jeans with holes results in an all-staff email from leadership informing everyone that holes in jeans are not professional workday attire. Guess what that little passive-aggressive email does? It sets gossip on fire. "You know the only reason we are getting that email is because Miss Walters is wearing holey jeans. She's too young for this job. She needs to grow up." Instead of confronting the one individual who may need to hear the message directly, leadership uses a more passive approach in order to avoid conflict. Conflict is not a dirty word or even necessarily a bad thing. It is, however, something that many administrators and teachers would like to avoid. The most useful and powerful tool a school culture can cultivate is empathy. Empathy approaches conflict from an understanding of the other person's feelings or experiences. Approaching conflict with empathy helps to defuse the situation. Below are basic tools you can start with to add empathy in your school:

- Understand the difference between empathy and sympathy. Sympathy is feeling sorry for someone. Empathy is recognizing the other person's feelings and putting yourself in their shoes.

- Use active listening with coworkers, parents, and students. Active listening means inquiring about the problem sincerely and acknowledging the other person's feelings and emotions.

- Approach conflict calmly. This is especially important when dealing with students' behaviors. Your job as an educator is to bring more calm into an already escalating situation.

Now, was I always an empathetic teacher? Nuh uh. I am still learning what empathy is and how to add more of it in my daily life (especially my home life with my own four little darlings).

Empathy is something you can water and grow. The biggest difference for me is learning to at least be more intentional with my listening and understanding. I am learning it is not always helpful to try to fix everything. As a mom and a teacher, I tend to want to put Band-Aids on owies. To make it all better. More times than not, the person who is having a hard time just wants to be heard and understood a little.

Like I mentioned, I was not always a model of empathy (and still far from it). When I first began teaching I did a pretty good job of avoiding gossip, cliques, and nastiness. In fact, so much so that my nickname became Schmitzerland. I was neutral. I wanted nothing to do with nastiness. Like many educators I did not want to engage in any sort of conflict, so I avoided it. If I heard others bullying or talking terribly about another teacher I didn't call them out on it. I just stayed away from that person or persons and hoped I wouldn't be their next target. But eventually I began partaking in this type of nastiness too. It did not feel good. It's not who I know I am meant to be but sadly

I joined on in. Clique mentality didn't leave many of us after we left junior high. But the root of the clique mentality when we were 13 is still the same thing that drives it now well into adulthood—fear.

Fear is what stokes the fire of negativity. The fear of being different. The fear of not being good enough. The fear of not making friends or being liked. The fear of being judged.

Mean girl (or guy) behavior is not the only form of negativity in a school. A negative attitude is what really adds fuel to the fire for negative school culture. Teachers who consistently complain and whine about everything are the ring leaders of this negative climate. Complaining is a quick road to nowhere, and negativity can breed fast. One of my favorite quotes about negativity is from Joyce Meyer: "Being negative only makes a difficult journey more difficult. You may be given a cactus, but you don't have to sit on it." Are you sitting on a cactus? Check below to see.

# HOW TO RECOGNIZE IF YOU ARE STOKING THE FLAMES OF NEGATIVITY

🔥 You complain all the time. About everything.

🔥 Change is your worst enemy. You fear change and are angry at anyone who suggests you change what you are doing.

🔥 You participate in gossip about your coworkers, the families you serve, or— worst yet—the kids you are serving.

🔥 You turn a blind eye to bullying. I am not talking about kids being bullied here. I mean staff bullying.

🔥 You have a clique and are exclusive to others.

🔥 You hate coming to work.

# HOW TO EXTINGUISH THE FLAMES

Not every moment of your teaching career will be filled with sunshine and lollipops. You will have down days. You will feel annoyed with demands from your school or district. You may become sick of your coworkers, the families you serve, and certain kids. These feelings are normal and allowed. You are human. The problem is when these feelings overcome you. When you become stuck in the flames of negativity is when action is needed. Here are a few steps on what you can begin doing today to douse your negative fire…

🔥 Find positive educators to interact with. Remember how you need that Work Wife? Make sure you are married to someone positive. There is a difference between venting and gossiping. If your work bestie only wants to gossip and be a downer you need to set a boundary.

🔥 Include the new teacher on the block. She/he may feel alone and isolated. Invite them to eat lunch with you or go for a coffee after school.

🔥 See change as an opportunity for growth and not something negative coming at you.

🔥 When you see or hear bullying behavior call out the bully. This is hard to do and most likely will put you in the path of a negative response, but we cannot continue to pretend like this type of behavior is okay.

🔥 Start organizing positive outings with your work family (e.g. go bowling, see a movie, have fun outside of school).

🔥 Stop allowing a negative climate to live and breathe in your school.

Negativity is contagious. A principal or school leadership member can try to set the tone for the building, but that only can do so much. It is truly up to the team to decide how much negative climate can live in a school. Isn't it much more enjoyable to go to work when it feels welcoming and good? Negativity is rooted in fear. The anecdote to fear is love. Love feels warm when you are surrounded by it. Negativity deteriorates your body and soul. An environment of love and inclusion is more productive and just plain feels better than an environment of nasty, fear, and gossip. Which would you prefer?

> "Clique mentality didn't leave many of us after we left junior high. But the root of the clique mentality when we were 13 is still the same thing that drives it now well into adulthood—fear."

# FLAME THROWING

### Stop Blaming and Start Collaborating

5

What is your why? Why are you an educator? If I could take a wild guess I will assume your answer deals directly with a desire to help kids and a belief in a positive future. Over the last two years I have interviewed hundreds of teachers, administrators, and policy makers. I wanted to get to the bottom of some of the discord in our schools. I asked many questions about challenges and successes. My favorite question I asked is:

*What is your why?* Guess what every single one of the participants' response was…. the kids. Students were at the core of each and every why. No matter what their role in education was, everyone responded to that question with basically the same answer.

If we are all on the same mission, why do we have so much flame throwing in the field? Teachers blame problems in the classroom on lack of support from administration. Administration blames lack of autonomy on policy makers. Policy makers blame lack of academic growth on teachers and administrators not following processes. The truth is we all want to do what is best for kids. We are on the same team. We need to spend less energy blaming each other and take more time collaborating and understanding that our mission is the same! The trick is having a little bit of empathy for each stakeholder.

It is time all educators decide to unite and ignite. And when I use the word educator I am using it in the sense of all involved in education (e.g. board members, teachers, policy makers, administrators). Uniting and igniting means all investors understand that all educators have good intentions at heart and are truly student centered. We all want success. We all want what is best for the kids. So…how do we do that?

Step 1: We must believe we are all on the same team.
Step 2: We must trust each other.

Blame and shame needs to go. The best way we can work together is through collaboration and empathy. The trust needs to go both ways. As teachers, we need our administrators and policy makers to trust that we are capable and professional enough to make decisions that are best for our students. But at the same time, we need to understand and acknowledge that our administrators and policy makers also have the students' best interests in mind when they are making their decisions and setting policies. Instead of assuming the worst about each other we need to start trusting that we are all on the same team. These are the keys to success. Below are some of the warning signs that you may be throwing flames instead of igniting collaboration.

## HOW TO RECOGNIZE WHEN YOU ARE THROWING FLAMES INSTEAD OF IGNITING COLLABORATION

🔥 When a change is suggested, you immediately turn on your defense mode and blame your administrator or policy maker.

🔥 You constantly speak negatively about your district and leadership.

🔥 You seek out others to complain to but never address an issue you have with leadership.

🔥 You are angry or concerned about things that directly affect your classroom/students but never take positive action to rectify your concerns.

# HOW TO
# EXTINGUSIH
# THE FLAMES

The key to collaboration is remembering our why. We are on the same team. Collaborating and empathizing does not mean you get what you want 100 percent of the time when you approach administration or leadership. It means that you feel heard, respected, and valued. If you have concerns and honestly try to collaborate and empathize with leadership but receive no response... you may want to consider that perhaps you are working in the wrong building or district. Be honest with yourself first before you make a big decision like leaving. Did you really try to connect and collaborate? Were you empathetic?

🔥 Start from a place of empathy. I talked
a little bit about being an empathetic
educator in the previous chapter, but it bears
repeating because of its value! Empathy is
understanding someone else's feelings or
views. Remember that we are all on the
same team and need to start acting like it.

🔥 If there is a policy you don't agree with
or fully understand ask for clarification
in a non-aggressive way. Again, come
from a place of collaboration instead of
immediately reaching out in attack mode.
Put down your pitchfork and put on your
listening ears.

🔥 Be an advocate for your classroom and
students. Be prepared to back your
advocacy with data and research. Data is
often the love language of policy makers.
If you can showcase that the proof is in
the pudding, it is much more likely that
administrators and leadership members
will be willing to listen to and consider
your point.

🔥 Invite others in. Ask your administrators/policymakers to visit your classroom to see what is happening and gain a better understanding of how they can best support you and your students. That is a huge part of what their job is.

🔥 Ask to shadow a leadership member. Just like you want them to better understand your role in education, you may want to understand more of what their job entails too. It may be different than you think.

You deserve to be heard, Teacher. Make sure you are hearing others too. To get churchy on you… "We are many parts. We are all one body. The gifts we have. We are given to share." Go share your gift. Ignite and light. We are one team. Start collaborating and empathizing. If the kids are truly our **WHY** in education, then being empathetic with each other is the place where we need to start to serve our students.

"The truth is we all want to do what is best for kids. We are on the same team. We need to spend less energy blaming each other and take more time collaborating and understanding that our mission is the same!"

# COME ON BABY LIGHT MY FIRE:

## How to Ignite Learning through Engagement and Relationships

In previous chapters we discussed the importance of collaboration and empathy. These are major stepping stones for supporting our students. Through collaboration and empathy for all stakeholders we are able to focus on our mission and our **WHY**...the kids. I firmly suggest you begin to start believing that your leadership team has positive intentions for supporting this mission. If you truly believe that leadership is not in it for the kids…then you are in the wrong place, friend. Make a change. Also believe that your coworkers are coming from a good place and start supporting them. Don't forget what I said about getting married…your Work Wife will be one of your best tools to keep the flames of burnout at bay. Collaborate and support your work spouse and team members. Once you have decided that everyone is on the same team it is time to begin with the real work… engagement.

Student engagement is the spark that will ignite the flames of learning. It is what makes the classroom glow. If students are not interested and engaged in what you are teaching it will result in both low academic and emotional learning outcomes. Student buy-in and interest are essential parts of learning. BUT! Before we begin to ignite and excite there is a very important element that must exist in your classroom…relationships.

I have a program evaluator bff named Abbey, who uses a great analogy for classroom expectations. Abbey says, "Classroom expectations are the backbone of the classroom." I have always loved this analogy and edu-stole it from her. I fully agree. Without solid expectations or strong organization in the classroom, the room falls apart in the same way that a spineless body would be a puddle of jelly. Expectations are so important. If classroom expectations are the spine or the backbone of your classroom, then relationships are the heart. You absolutely cannot get anything accomplished if your students don't truly believe that you at least like them, if not love them. When students feel secure and safe in the classroom they will work for the teacher. I love the quote, "Before we Bloom we must Maslow." This means if you want to implement higher-order thinking skills from Bloom's Taxonomy in your room you better make sure you have met students' needs from Maslow's Hierarchy of Needs. In other words,…rigor is important, but relationships are king!

So how do we build strong relationships with our students? What steps do we take? Well for starters, make sure they believe you are a person in their corner. That is the groundwork that must begin to happen. Below are five other strategies on how you can *begin* to build authentic and genuine relationships with your students…

1. **Home visits and phone calls.** I would highly suggest you make the time to either visit where your students live or make a phone call home to their parents/ guardians. When I was teaching, I would carve out a week each summer before school began to go on home visits to every student I had the correct phone number for. I would allow 15 minutes per kiddo and go to their home to meet the family and read a short book. I was not paid extra money to go on these home visits, but I felt so strongly about the power they possessed that I did them anyway! The power of the home visit is it instantly starts the groundwork for building a positive relationship with the family and the student. You can learn a lot about a students' home life in a short 15-minute

visit. If home visits are not something you are able to do or comfortable doing I would suggest making phone calls throughout the school year. Make sure the intent of the phone call is to only share something positive about the students. "Hi Mrs. Jones. I wanted to call to let you know that Jamal has been working so hard during independent work time. He has been on task all week!" Parents and students love to receive these phone calls and typically are shocked and delighted.

2. **Be authentic and genuine.** This may seem like a no-brainer, but I think we as educators need a good reminder to do this sometimes. Being authentic and genuine includes smiling, making eye contact, and having social conversations with students. Allow time for students to TALK to you and you talk to them. Teaching can be hard and overwhelming. We often are so concerned and worried about meeting standards and preparing for assessments that we forget this very important part

of our job! We must make the time to be sensitive and aware of not only the academic needs of our students but their emotional needs as well! They are both equally important.

3. **Play games, sing songs, team build, be silly.** Making the time to build a classroom community is so important! Kids LOVE to sing with you. If you aren't a singer and that's not your style, make sure you are doing other things to build your classroom team! Play games. Be silly. Remember 10-15 years ago when the buzz phrase for educators was: *creating lifelong learners*? Guess what promotes lifelong learners? Kids that LOVE learning. Make school fun! If your principal comes into your classroom and sees you playing games with your kids make sure and tell him/her that you are creating lifelong learners. What we need more of is creative thinkers instead of cookie cutter thinkers! Fostering an environment where your students feel safe to take risks and have

fun with learning will promote creative thinking. We need to bring joy back into our students' journeys.

4. **Allow students to have ownership of the room.** Here is the deal… Pinterest decorated classrooms are lovely and fun. Classroom themes are cute. However, they in no way dictate whether or not you are an effective teacher. They simply show if you're a crafty guy or gal. I would suggest leaving a large chunk of your classroom open for the students to decide how the space should be used. Make sure to leave plenty of room on your walls for student work! Instead of choosing a classroom theme you may even want to allow your students the opportunity to choose a fun theme. When students feel like they are valued decision makers in the classroom they feel proud and will take better care of the materials and the room! It is a very doable way to give the students even more ownership of the classroom and their learning. It fosters

an environment that says, "This is OUR class" versus "This is MY class".

5. **Develop classroom expectations together.** This one fits right along with number 4. It is about giving autonomy and ownership back to your students. Eliciting their ideas and views about appropriate classroom expectations will go a long way towards securing students' buy-in to how the classroom is run. Now of course there may be some expectations that you as a teacher or as a school already have in place and those expectations are non-negotiable. That is fine! Just make sure you are still asking your students as a group what they see as valuable and reasonable expectations in the classroom. Like I mentioned…classroom expectations are the spine. The easiest way to help support effective behavior management is through authentic and real relationships with your students.

Now that you have some ideas and strategies on how to build solid relationships and remember why relationships are important, you can begin to self-assess the level of engagement that you are implementing for your students. Teachers can easily fall into a trap of implementing low-level engagement lessons in the classroom. Read below to check where you are.

# HOW TO RECOGNIZE THE FLAMES OF LOW-LEVEL ENGAGNEMNT IN YOUR CLASSROOM

- You teach the same lessons year after year regardless of students' abilities or interests.
- You strictly follow a pacing guide and continue with lessons no matter if the students find the lessons too easy or have a lack of understanding.
- You choose all elements and structures of the classroom (i.e. classroom setup, expectations, content).
- Most of the content you teach is rote and leaves little room for students to develop creative thinking skills.

🔥 You rarely take the time to engage in social conversations, team build, smile, or be silly with your students.

Getting in a rut is easy to do. I know when the flames of burnout were really encompassing me I could check off almost all of the warning signs above for low-level engagement. The good news is once you start to be real with yourself and truly self-reflect without blaming others, you can begin to douse these flames. Teacher, start to consider at least trying some of the steps below to support high levels of student engagement.

# HOW TO EXTINGUISH THE FLAMES

Start getting creative in the lessons you implement! Guess what…curriculum companies are a business. They are meant to make money and should be used as a suggested guide on how to teach. The designers of the curriculum don't know your students. YOU know your students. YOU are a professional. Get a firm grasp of what the state standards are and begin creating lessons based on those standards. Forcing teachers to follow a scripted curriculum is like making Wolfgang Puck make Mac-N-Cheese from the blue box. Yeah, he can do it, but wouldn't you rather eat something he makes from scratch?

🔥 A pacing guide is just that…a guide. If students don't understand a lesson… reteach it. If students already have a firm grasp of a concept…move ahead! Again, you are a professional. Use your judgment to engage your kids! Don't get hung up on what the guide says you should be doing each week or month.

🔥 Give your students voice and choice in the classroom. Sheesh. Let go of the reigns a little, Teacher. If you want engagement to be high, allow students to have a vested interest in what is happening in the classroom. Watch how differently they behave and interact when they have ownership of their learning.

🔥 Implement more lessons that encourage creative thinking versus producing cookie cutter results. Worksheets produce cookie cutter results. There. I said it. Sure, worksheets could have a place in your room for some low-level forms of practicing skills, but they should not be what you rely on in your day-to-day instruction. There is, however, a difference between a worksheet and a recording sheet. If you give each student the same worksheet all results should be the same. If you give each student a recording sheet, results can be creative and varied. Want to increase engagement? Decrease your number of worksheets and use more recording sheets.

Stop taking yourself so seriously. Be silly with your students and enjoy the experience of being a teacher! You are with your kids for a huge chunk of their day. You are one of the most influential people in their lives. If you have programmed yourself to be in robot mode in the classroom, you are depriving both your students and yourself from having a joyful classroom experience.

You may notice that many of the above suggestions to extinguish the flames of low-level engagement are similar to what I suggested for building engaging relationships. That is because relationship building and promoting high student engagement go hand in hand! Do some soul searching, and start having fun as an educator. Remember why you are here!

"Curriculum companies are a business. They are meant to make money and should be used as a suggested guide on how to teach. The designers of the curriculum don't know your students. YOU know your students. YOU are a professional. Get a firm grasp of what the state standards are and begin creating lessons based on those standards."

# FIRE BREATHING MONSTER

## Stop Teacher-to-Student Negativity in your School

Since we just discussed the power of positive relationships and engagement in your classroom, I want to flip the coin on you and talk about a topic that is sure to make you wiggle a little bit uncomfortably in your seat...let's get real about teacher negativity towards students.

Teacher-to-student negativity is a very real and dark cloud that lives in almost every single school across the country. Let me clarify what

I mean by teacher-to-student negativity.... I am not talking about a harsh redirection every once in a while or a stern look here or there. When I am talking about teacher-to-student negativity in this chapter I mean a sustained, nasty way of a teacher treating students. I mean threats, yelling, sarcasm, frowning, eye rolling, and an overall miserable demeanor towards your students. Yeah. Let's go there. This behavior needs to be addressed.

I want you to think back on all of your years in school and try to remember the different teachers you had throughout. Your most memorable teachers made some sort of impact on you. It will either be a negative impact or a positive one. Now I want you to pinpoint a teacher who encompassed the teacher-to-student negativity that you just read about. Think of the teacher who was absolutely miserable in the classroom and made your life miserable too. I can see my third-grade teacher as clear as day. I can remember exact phrases she used (e.g., "Can't you see it? The directions are on the board! What are you, stupid?"). I see her angry face. I remember how uncomfortable I felt in her classroom. I can even remember where I sat. Guess what…I was a good student. I was shy and a rule follower. None of her negative threats or consequences were ever given specifically to me, but they impacted me so much that I can clearly remember them. Just think of the impact she had on the children on the receiving end of her direct nastiness! I was in third grade 30 years ago. That's how impactful a negative teacher is.

I am so sick of this behavior you guys. As teachers we have allowed this to live and breathe in our schools forever. We are complicit. I am 100 percent guilty of being complicit to this type of behavior when I was a classroom teacher. When I saw this happening in the school I taught in, I turned a completely blind eye. If a teacher was in the hall reaming and yelling at her class I walked on by without making eye contact with the teacher. I remember thinking... *"Man! I am not saying anything to her. I am scared of her. I sure hope none of my kindergarteners have to her as their teacher."* This is a perfect example of how we are being complicit to this type of negativity as educators. None of us want to be the snitch. We also typically don't like confrontation, so we allow it to continue at the expense of our students.

Again…let me be clear. I am not talking about redirections or consequences (although it can sometimes be linked to the delivery of these actions). What I am referring to is a sustained pattern of negativity from the teacher towards his or her students. Read below to identify teacher-to-student negativity and double check that you are not engaging in these types of behavior.

# HOW TO RECOGNIZE TEACHER-TO-STUDENT NEGATIVITY

🔥 The teacher has a generally miserable "I hate my job" type of attitude in the classroom.

🔥 You observe any of the following from yourself or a coworker: frowning, a flat affect, a lack of enthusiasm.

🔥 Yelling and screaming can frequently be heard from the classroom. Sometimes it is directed to an individual student or sometimes it could be directed towards an entire group of students.

🔥 Sarcasm is often used in the classroom

## DISCLAIMER

Sarcasm may be used briefly in classrooms of older students who understand the intent. However, sarcasm should never be used to embarrass a student, and it definitely should never be used in an early childhood classroom - remember early childhood includes birth through third grade. Young children do not understand sarcasm.

🔥 Other teachers are uncomfortable around the teacher who is spreading a negative teacher-to-student environment.

🔥 The kids are afraid or uncomfortable in the classroom. Students rarely approach the teacher even when they need him or her because they are scared or there is a lack of relationship present.

Blech, right?! I know you see this. You know it is living in your school! We cannot continue to idly sit back and watch this type of fire breathing monster encompass our kids. I now consider myself a mandatory reporter of teacher-to-student negativity. You should be too. Here is what you do to help.

# HOW TO EXTINGUISH THE FLAMES

Okay, first of all, if you recognize that I am describing you or consistent parts of your behavior…take a breath. You can overcome this. Reach out for help from someone at your school who you trust and who is in your corner. Start reflecting on your **WHY** again. Why are you a teacher? Most likely you are overwhelmed with something in your classroom or personal life. This however does not give you an excuse to treat students this way. If you need support, go find it! Asking for help is definitely not a sign of weakness. If you are too afraid to ask for help, or if you have tried to change but inevitably

veer back into the same patterns of
negativity towards your students, then it
is probably time to go. I know that may
be hard to hear—but the fact is if you are
unable to treat students with respect and
compassion they deserve, then you need
to remove yourself from the classroom.

 Stop being complicit. If you see this type
of behavior in your school from other
teachers, you need to address it. If you
are not comfortable approaching your
coworker directly you need to seek out
someone in a leadership position who
will. You know the phrase "snitches get
stitches"?...this does not apply when we
are dealing with our students. It is your
job to be a student advocate. You must
be a voice for the voiceless. The five-year
old is not going to go home and say,
"Moooooom….my teacher is using a
lot of sarcasm and screams at our class
frequently. I think she needs support."
You, Teacher. You are the one who needs
to advocate for all students in your

building, not just the students you are serving in your classroom.

🔥 Reach out to your coworkers and offer to help and support them without judgment. Show compassion and empathy for each other. Most of the time the teacher portraying this behavior has some serious stuff going on…again it is not an excuse but offer to help in a nonjudgmental way!

Teacher, the power is in YOUR hands to decide your attitude in the classroom. It is also up to you to begin objecting to this type of behavior in your school. Silence is compliance. Our kids deserve better. Every child in the school is *your* kid, not just the ones enrolled in your classroom. Start fighting for your kids.

> "We cannot continue to idly sit back and watch this type of fire breathing monster encompass our kids."

# TOO MANY IRONS IN THE FIRE

8

## Choosing Self-care over Self-sacrifice

There were many ignitors that fanned my flames of burnout while I was a classroom teacher, but if I were to pick the greatest source of fuel to my fire it would be my lack of self-care while I was teaching. I have a feeling that is true for many of you too. And that is why I have saved this important chapter for last.

Taking care of everyone else's needs before my own was like pouring gasoline on an already growing flame. When working in a high-stress job such as teaching, guilt about taking care of YOU should not be something that you add to your already full plate. Self-care is not selfish. You absolutely cannot serve effectively as a teacher if you are not prioritizing taking care of yourself along with meeting the needs of your students and families.

Self-care is hugely important for any teacher. But because it is so near and dear to my heart and own personal experience (and because there are so many of you out there), I want to take a moment to talk specifically to you, Teacher Mama....

Mamas...I see you. I see you taking care of other people's children. I see you missing the first day of school for your own child to be in your classroom. I see you missing their field trips, concerts, and lunch dates because you are a public servant. I see you grading papers at soccer practice after working all day. I see you scrambling to organize dinner and keep up with the laundry when you are dead ass tired. I see you trying to be everything to everyone while putting yourself very last on your list. When you come home from teaching after a long day there is no break from children or trying to meet the needs of the needy.

Teacher Mamas...I know you love your babies with all your heart. Your heart is especially unique because you hold not only the love for your own children but extreme love for other people's children too. They are your kids for a school year and beyond. But in order for you to be the best teacher and mom that you can be it is essential to realize the value of self-care. You also must stop putting up a façade that life is perfect and you can do it all. I blame social media for fanning that flame. Facebook pictures are often staged. Instagram has lots of cool filters. When we see the lives of others through these filtered, staged pics we begin comparing ourselves to a messed-up version of reality. Stop comparing and do more self-caring.

# RECOGNIZING WHEN YOU FEEL THE BURN OF A LACK OF SELF-CARE

Somehow, we have decided as a society that the more you work the better you are. Coming in to school early and staying late must equate to you being an excellent, dedicated teacher. A former principal would often remind us as a staff that there is a difference between working hard and working smart. Of course, there will be days when a few extra hours at school are beneficial and essential. Just make sure you're being smart about it. Are you burning the candle at both ends? Look below to see.

🔥 You put the needs of everyone else before your own (e.g. students, spouse, offspring, coworkers, parents).

🔥 You work extreme hours while at school. You are the first to arrive and the last to leave.

🔥 You bring hours of work home each night.

- You are tired, moody, and often angry. You may snap at the ones you love the most.

- You always say, "Yes" even when you do not want to.

- You have stopped taking care of your health and eat food that is bad for you. This includes medicating your stress with alcohol, fast food, or treats.

- You get less than seven hours of sleep each night.

- You do not exercise or barely at all.

- You have no time for hobbies or extracurricular activities.

- You rarely do anything that you love to do.

# HOW TO EXTINGUISH THE FLAMES

Without a doubt, some of the symptoms from the above list will happen throughout your school year and throughout your life. Being a teacher does not mean you are not a human. What you want to do is self-check your self-care. How often are you bringing home work each night? Do you often feel angry at school and/or at home? Are you a doormat for others? Do you always say yes? These are self-sabotaging behaviors. Self-care is the opposite of self-sabotage. There are many strategies to douse the self-sabotaging flames. Below are a few ideas to get you started.

🔥 Do something little for yourself each day. It does not need to be anything that costs any money (e.g. go for a walk, call your sister, meditate, spend time with your pet, take a bath).

🔥 Check in with your feelings. First accept that you feel angry, sad, or upset. Those feelings are okay to feel! Next, allow the feelings to go when they are ready to leave you. If you are holding onto anger, sadness, or regret each day that is when they become problematic and when you may need to seek additional resources to help with those feelings (e.g. therapy or your doctor).

🔥 Ask for help when you need it. You do not have to be Wonder Woman or Super Man. It is okay to admit you are struggling and need a little help. That does not make you less of a teacher or parent.

🔥 Connect with your friends or Work Wife. Laughing and having fun with people you love really is a good medicine.

🔥 Drink water. Seriously. Quit the Diet Coke. Fill your body with things that are good for you!

🔥 Go to bed earlier. Sleep is self-care.

🔥 Exercise daily. This doesn't mean you have to be a CrossFit hero, but you should move your body and take care of yourself somehow each day. Teacher, go for a walk!

🔥 Say NO without giving an explanation or an apology. You don't need to be rude about it but saying no to things that deplete you is a form of self-care.

Teachers live a life of service. You are serving the needs of students, families, and your school family. Teachers serve our community and our future. Having a career or vocation in service is a gift. Focusing on self-care does not mean you have lost sight of your purpose as an educator. It simply means you are recharging your own battery so that you have the energy to be a more powerful light in our world.

"Self-care is not selfish.
You absolutely cannot
serve effectively as a
teacher if you are not
prioritizing taking care
of yourself along with
meeting the needs of
your students
and families."

## STOP, DROP, AND ROLL

### Extinguish or Evacuate

Okay…time to get real. We just discussed eight common causes that lead to teachers going up in flames and I provided you with some basic starting points on how to extinguish these flames. Now it is going to be up to you, Teacher, to decide where your future leads.

My goal with this book was to help you recognize when you might be in the midst of burnout and provide you with essential tips and strategies to douse those flames so that you can continue to find joy in your journey and your job! However if, after doing a lot of soul searching and self-reflecting, you still find yourself up in flames that just won't go out, do not be too hard on yourself! Taking a break and leaving teaching was the best move I could have made professionally and personally. I knew I needed to go even though it was extremely scary and heartbreaking to leave. Also understand that you can always take time away and then come back. There are many opportunities for educators to still work in the field of education and not necessarily be a classroom teacher. Explore other avenues! If the burn is too much, go take the time to learn some new things. You will be even better for it and for your future students will benefit when/ if you do return!

Being a teacher is truly a calling. I believe the students placed in your room are placed there either because they need you or you need them. Either way there is a reason why you are together for a short year. Soak it up! Remember to reflect on your **WHY**, resist the urge to conform while still being open to change, marry your Work Wife, celebrate and collaborate with your coworkers, douse the flames of negativity, ignite and excite your students with genuine relationships and engagement, be an advocate for your students by dousing teacher-to-student negativity, and maybe most importantly fan the flames of self-care.

Colleen

Need a little extra help? Let's have a hydrant party! Contact Colleen for recharging professional development sessions to help your staff acknowledge and extinguish the flames of burnout: www.colleenschmit.com

# ABOUT THE AUTHOR

Colleen Schmit is the author of *Crisscross Applesauce and Shut the Hell Up: 10 Reflective Lessons for New and Seasoned Teachers.* She earned her master's in early childhood education at Concordia University, and began her career as an educator of young children in Omaha, NE. Today, Colleen is an early childhood consultant, speaker, and program evaluator. She loves helping teachers reclaim their spark for teaching. Colleen and her husband, Bob, enjoy spending time playing with their four young kiddos and eating lots of pizza.

# ACKNOWLEDGMENTS

To my own four little monkeys, Kaitlyn, Scarlett, Will, and Delaney. I am so thankful you choose me to be your mama. I am the luckiest.

A special thanks to my live-in editor-in-chief, Bob. Schmove Schmou!

Thank you to my supportive PLN! A giant shout out to all of the amazing educators on #ecechat. Jessica Cabeen, Heidi Veal, Nancy Alvarez, and Katy Phinney—you are powerhouses in the field of early childhood education. Thank you for being models of advocacy for young children.

Thank you to Rachel Moore! Your skillz are impressive and I am so grateful for your help.

Finally, a thank you to Omaha Public Schools. I am eternally grateful for my experiences working in the district and serving the children and families of South Omaha.

52141553R00074

Made in the USA
Columbia, SC
27 February 2019